# NAKED
# Mole-Rats

by Emily Hudd

**Content Consultant**
Stan Braude, PhD, Teaching Professor
College of Arts & Sciences
Washington University in St. Louis

CAPSTONE PRESS
a capstone imprint

Bright Idea Books are published by Capstone Press
1710 Roe Crest Drive, North Mankato, Minnesota 56003
www.mycapstone.com

**Library of Congress Cataloging-in-Publication Data**
Names: Hudd, Emily, author.
Title: Naked mole-rats / by Emily Hudd.
Description: North Mankato, Minnesota : Capstone Press, [2020] | Series:
   Unique animal adaptations | Audience: Grade 4 to 6. | Includes
   bibliographical references and index.
Identifiers: LCCN 2018061085 (print) | LCCN 2018061650 (ebook) | ISBN
   9781543571769 (ebook) | ISBN 9781543571615 (hardcover) | ISBN 9781543575101 (paperback)
Subjects: LCSH: Naked mole rat--Juvenile literature. | Naked mole
   rat--Adaptation--Juvenile literature.
Classification: LCC QL737.R628 (ebook) | LCC QL737.R628 H83 2020 (print) | DDC 599.35--dc23
LC record available at https://lccn.loc.gov/2018061085

All internet sites appearing in back matter were available and accurate when this book was sent
to press.

**Editorial Credits**
Editor: Marie Pearson
Designer: Becky Daum
Production Specialist: Colleen McLaren

**Photo Credits**
Shutterstock Images: belizar, 21, Neil Bromhall, cover, 5, 6–7, 8–9, 11, 12–13, 14–15, 16–17, 18–19,
22–23, 24–25, 28, 31, Taylorbear, 27

Design Elements: Shutterstock Images

Printed in the United States of America.
PA70

# TABLE OF CONTENTS

# CHAPTER 1

# PINK
# Rodents

Is that a hairless rat? No, it's a naked mole-rat! They are **native** to warm deserts in East Africa. They live underground. Many also live in zoos around the world. They look hairless. They are **rodents**. But they are not rats.

# HAIRS

Naked mole-rats have about 100 tiny hairs on their bodies.

Naked mole-rats are almost hairless. But they do have whiskers.

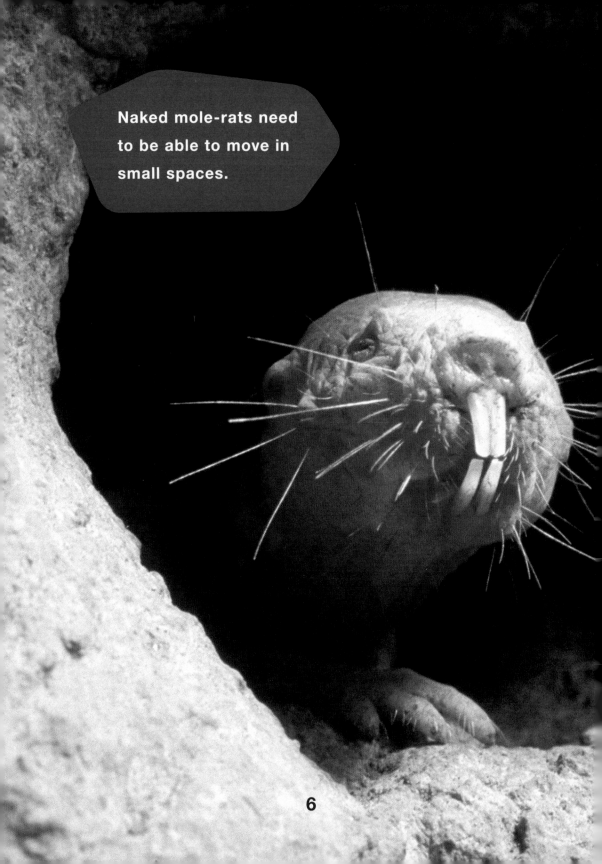

Naked mole-rats need to be able to move in small spaces.

Naked mole-rats have pink, wrinkled bodies. Most are 3 to 4 inches (8 to 10 centimeters) long. They weigh 1 to 1.8 ounces (30 to 50 grams). Their tails can be up to 3 inches (8 cm) long.

The wrinkles are from extra skin. The mole-rats need to turn around in tight spaces. They bend their bodies. Having loose skin makes moving around easier.

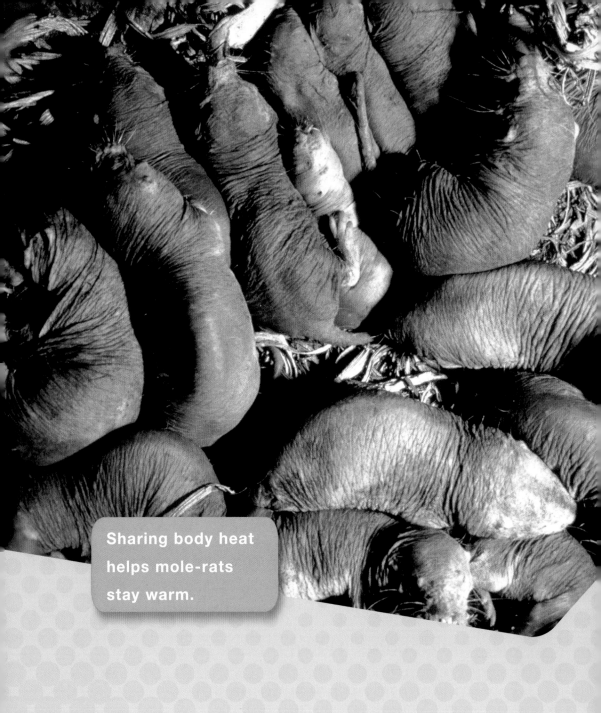

Sharing body heat helps mole-rats stay warm.

Desert nights are cold. Naked mole-rats need help staying warm. Sometimes they sleep on top of each other in piles. They share body heat. When they pile together, the temperature in their home stays about 86 degrees Fahrenheit (3 degrees Celsius).

# CHAPTER 2

# ADAPTATIONS

Naked mole-rats have amazing **adaptations**. They have tiny eyes. They cannot see well. They rely on their sense of smell. It helps them find food. They also rely on their sense of touch. They can feel **vibrations** in the ground.

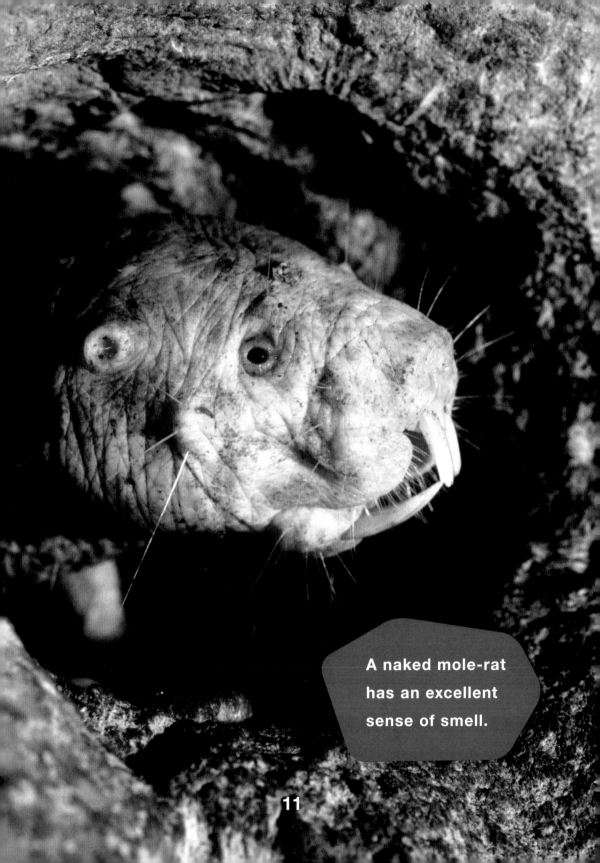

A naked mole-rat has an excellent sense of smell.

Naked mole-rats have **sensitive** whiskers on their faces and tails. Whiskers help the rats know where they are. The stiff hairs brush against tunnel walls. The mole-rats don't run into the walls.

Whiskers help naked mole-rats in their underground habitat.

Mole-rats have hairs between their toes. The hairs help sweep soil when the mole-rats dig.

These animals have four big front teeth. Two are on the top. Two are on the bottom. Their teeth grow outside of their mouths. Their lips close behind their teeth. Dirt stays out of their mouths as they dig. Strong jaws help them dig **burrows**.

A naked mole-rat uses
its teeth and feet to dig.

Their jaws and teeth are strong. They can chew through hard ground. They can even chew through concrete! The teeth never stop growing. Chewing grinds down the teeth. It keeps them from growing too long.

## TUNNELS

A naked mole-rat digs tunnels about 1.5 inches (4 cm) wide.

Naked mole-rats eat roots. They find the roots underground. They do not drink. Their food gives them the water they need.

Naked mole-rats gather roots in their burrows.

Most living things need oxygen to live. Oxygen is a gas. Humans can live only six minutes without it. Naked mole-rats can live up to 18 minutes without it. This helps them survive when they pile together. There is less oxygen at the bottom of the pile.

Naked mole-rats at the bottom of a pile can tolerate getting less oxygen.

# CHAPTER 3

# LIFE
# Cycle

Naked mole-rats live in groups. Each group is a family. One **female** is the queen. She is the biggest. She weighs twice as much as some of the other mole-rats. The queen is the only one in the **colony** to have babies. The babies are called pups.

The queen has up to 30 pups at one time. She can give birth four times in one year. At three or four weeks old, the pups can start working.

Naked mole-rat pups are born helpless.

Some adult mole-rats watch after the pups.

Naked mole-rats **cooperate**. They work together to dig and clean tunnels. Some care for the queen. Some take care of the pups. Some find food.

Large mole-rats may protect the colony. They can block the tunnel. They keep snakes from getting in. Sometimes they protect their colony from other colonies. They keep the queen and pups safe. Workers are all brothers and sisters.

## BIG COLONIES

Most naked mole-rat colonies have 70 mole-rats. The largest colony **scientists** found had 295.

The burrow has different areas.

Naked mole-rats sleep in one area.

They poop and pee in another.

Tunnels connect all the areas.

Tunnels lead to wide chambers.

Naked mole-rats live longer than any other rodent. They can live up to 30 years in zoos. Scientists don't know how long they live in the wild.

# CHAPTER 4

# MOLE-RATS AND
# Humans

Naked mole-rats are not in danger at this time. Some eat crops. Farmers may consider them pests. But most mole-rats live in places where there is little human influence.

Others live in zoos. Scientists and visitors can watch naked mole-rats at the zoo. They can see the amazing ways a colony works together.

**Zoos can make mole-rat habitats that allow scientists to observe the animals.**

# GLOSSARY

**adaptation**
a behavior or body part that helps an animal survive in its environment

**burrow**
a hole underground where animals live

**colony**
a family of naked mole-rats

**cooperate**
to work together

**female**
an animal that can give birth to young animals or lay eggs

**native**
from a certain area

**rodent**
a mammal with long front teeth used for gnawing; rats, mice, and squirrels are rodents

**scientist**
a person who studies the world around us

**sensitive**
noticing small changes, feelings, or smells

**vibration**
a small movement

# TRIVIA

1. In most mammals, nerves are cells that tell the brain when the body gets a cut or bruise. A naked mole-rat's nerves are different from a human's. They do not send those signals. So naked mole-rats cannot feel many things that are painful to people.

2. Adult naked mole-rats have special bacteria in their bodies. The bacteria help them digest food. Young naked mole-rats eat the poop of older mole-rats. The bacteria they need is in the poop.

3. Two-year-old mole-rats start new colonies. They leave the safety of their burrow at night. They can run more than 1 mile (1.6 kilometers) away. When they find a partner from a different colony, they dig into the ground and start a new burrow.

# ACTIVITY

## USE YOUR SENSES

Naked mole-rats use their whiskers and sense of smell to get around. Imagine you have to navigate your home like a naked mole-rat. Ask a friend to help you place a blindfold on and keep you safe. Now, walk around your home. How do you know what room you are in? Does it smell different than the other rooms? Can you use your fingers, hands, feet, or toes like whiskers? How does the floor feel? Are there objects in the room that give you clues? Explain how you navigated your home and found different areas. Then, try this activity with some family or friends. Is it more challenging with a group?

# FURTHER RESOURCES

**Want to learn more about rodents?**
**Dig into these resources:**

Rake, Jody Sullivan. *Meerkats, Moles, and Voles. Animals of the Underground.* Underground Safari. North Mankato, Minn.: Capstone Press, 2016.

Rake, Jody Sullivan. *Star-Nosed Moles and Other Extreme Mammal Adaptations.* Extreme Adaptations. North Mankato, Minn.: Capstone Press, 2014.

Smithsonian's National Zoo & Conservation Biology Institute:
Naked Mole-Rat Cam
https://nationalzoo.si.edu/webcams/naked-mole-rat-cam

Zoo Atlanta: Naked Mole Rat
https://zooatlanta.org/animal/naked-mole-rat/

**Ready to find out about other animal adaptations?**
**Learn more here:**

Gagne, Tammy. *The Strangest Animals in the World.* All About Animals. North Mankato, Minn.: Capstone Press, 2015.

PBS NatureWorks: Structural and Behavioral Adaptations
https://nhpbs.org/natureworks/nwep1.htm

# INDEX